lonely planet Kids™

Marco's MAZE MISSION

Jane Gledhill

Hi, I'm **MARCO!**

And I'm **AMELIA!**

Help us travel a world
of mazes on a special mission,
and discover amazing facts along the way.
Are you up to the challenge? Then let's go!

CAN YOU HELP?

ARRIVALS

Disaster! Famous photographer and friend of Lonely Planet, Geronimo Keats, has just returned to London from a round-the-world expedition. But it looks like the locks on his luggage have broken and he has lost most of his equipment along the way!

GERONIMO
Lonely Planet? I've got a serious problem. Can you help?

Luckily, he knows just who to call... two young explorers who are perfect for the job. Lonely Planet to the rescue!

2

AT LONELY PLANET HQ

Amelia and Marco have been called in to HQ to help solve this international mystery. But they'll need your help!

LONELY PLANET BOSS
Marco, head to the airport and get on the next flight to Oslo. We need you to find Geronimo's belongings before someone else does! Amelia, stay at HQ with Geronimo, and help Marco retrace Geronimo's steps. Use your tablets to keep in touch.

AMELIA
Got it, boss!

MARCO
Don't worry, Geronimo. You can count on us! We'll have your lost things back with you in no time.

GERONIMO
Thank you, Marco!

SECURITY SLALOM

MARCO: Hi Amelia! I'm at the airport. Anything you need me to look for here?

AMELIA: Yes. Geronimo said he was pulled aside for a check at security. We're thinking maybe they didn't put everything back in his bag.

MARCO: Good idea. I'll take a look!

1 Continue the route at the next dotted arrow.

START HERE!

Weave in and out of the security line to find what Geronimo left behind. Make sure you go through each area in order!

FLUMMOX RATING

3

Stuck? Solution on Page 88

Continue the route at the next dotted arrow.

2

3

END HERE!

5

MARCO: Hey Amelia, I found a camera at the airport! I'm now in Oslo. Where do I need to go first?

AMELIA: Head to Vigeland Park to meet Geronimo's friend, Leif Berg.

MARCO: Will do!

Help Marco through the stone statues in the park to find Geronimo's friend Leif Berg.

START HERE!

FLUMMOX RATING

4

Stuck? Solution on Page 88

VIGELAND ADVENTURE!

The Vigeland Sculpture Park was completed in 1949. It has over 200 statues made by the artist Gustav Vigeland. The statues are made from stone, bronze, or iron.

HIDDEN GEM

The Vigeland Sculpture Park is in the middle of Frogner Park, the biggest park in central Oslo. As well as the Vigeland Sculpture Park, Frogner Park is also home to the biggest children's playground in Norway.

END HERE!

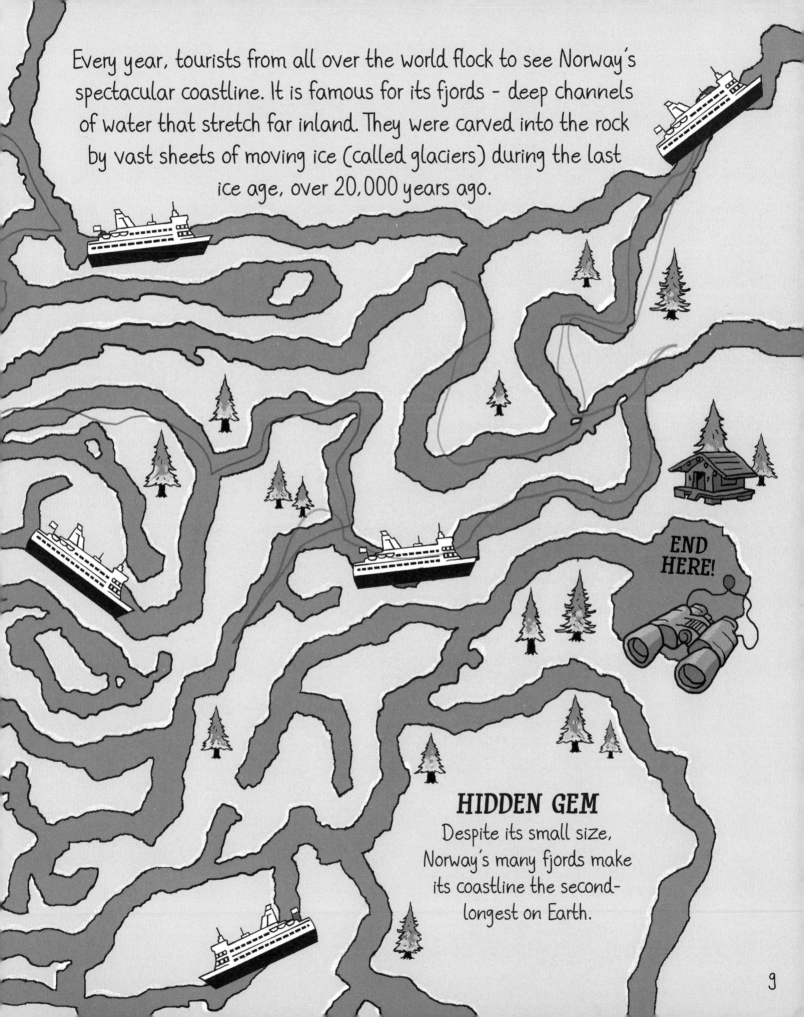

Every year, tourists from all over the world flock to see Norway's spectacular coastline. It is famous for its fjords - deep channels of water that stretch far inland. They were carved into the rock by vast sheets of moving ice (called glaciers) during the last ice age, over 20,000 years ago.

END HERE!

HIDDEN GEM
Despite its small size, Norway's many fjords make its coastline the second-longest on Earth.

END HERE!

FLUMMOX RATING
3
Stuck? Solution on Page 88

AMELIA: How were the fjords? Find anything?

MARCO: Yes, binoculars! Where next, Amelia?

AMELIA: Russia! Meet Geronimo's assistant, Natalia Kedrov, at a metro station in St. Petersburg. She and Geronimo did a shoot at St. Basil's Cathedral in Moscow.

MARCO: On my way!

The St. Petersburg Metro in Russia is the deepest subway system in the world, with 50 of its stations located over 98 feet (30 m) underground.

CATHEDRAL CAPER

St. Basil's Cathedral is located in Moscow's Red Square. It was built by Ivan the Terrible and was completed in 1560. Its towers and multicolored domes are shaped like the flames of a bonfire rising into the sky.

START HERE!

NATALIA
Hello Marco! I worked with Geronimo on a shoot at St. Basil's Cathedral, and then we had lunch at a café nearby.

MARCO
Thanks Natalia, let's check out both places. Geronimo thinks he may have forgotten something.

After a quick stop for a drink at the café, zigzag around the cathedral to discover what Geronimo lost in Moscow.

Stuck? Solution on Page 89

13

CHOCOLATE TIME!

Belgian chocolate is some of the most delicious chocolate on the planet. Every year, Belgian factories make over 187,400 tons of it to fill Belgium's 2,000 chocolate shops and to export all over the world.

CHOCOLATE GIFTS

HIDDEN GEM
The first chocolates in Belgium were made by pharmacists and sold as a type of medicine.

END HERE!

FOREST FORAY!

MARGO: Wow! That was deee-licious. And I found Geronimo's lens bag.

AMELIA: Hope you saved some for me! Right, now you're off to Germany. Geronimo's cousin, Hans Hofmann, owns a campsite deep in the Black Forest. Geronimo stayed there on his last trip.

MARGO: On my way!

The Black Forest, or *Schwarzwald* in German, is named for the evergreen trees that form a dark canopy over the forest floor. Many stories, such as Hansel and Gretel, are set here.

START HERE!

Weave in and out of the woods to find Hans Hofmann's campsite. Look for Hansel and Gretel along the way!

FLUMMOX RATING

2

Stuck? Solution on Page 89

HIDDEN GEM
Cuckoo clocks have been made in the Black Forest region since the 18th century.

END HERE!

TURRET TANGLE

The beautiful Hohenzollern Castle perches on top of a hill near the Black Forest. The castle you see today was completed in 1867, but previous versions have stood on the site since 1061.

MARCO
Hi Hans! I'm a friend of your cousin, Geronimo. He thinks he lost something when he last saw you. Do you know where?

HANS
We had a fun trip climbing the battlements of Hohenzollern Castle. Let's go take a look. Hope you like heights!

START HERE!

Help Hans and Marco climb the battlements of Hohenzollern Castle to see what Geronimo lost. Watch out for the White Lady!

HIDDEN GEM

The White Lady is the ghost of a widow who haunts Hohenzollern Castle. Legend has it that after the death of her husband, the White Lady murdered her two children in order to find a new husband. She is said to bring disaster to anyone who sees her.

FLUMMOX RATING

3

Stuck? Solution on Page 89

END HERE!

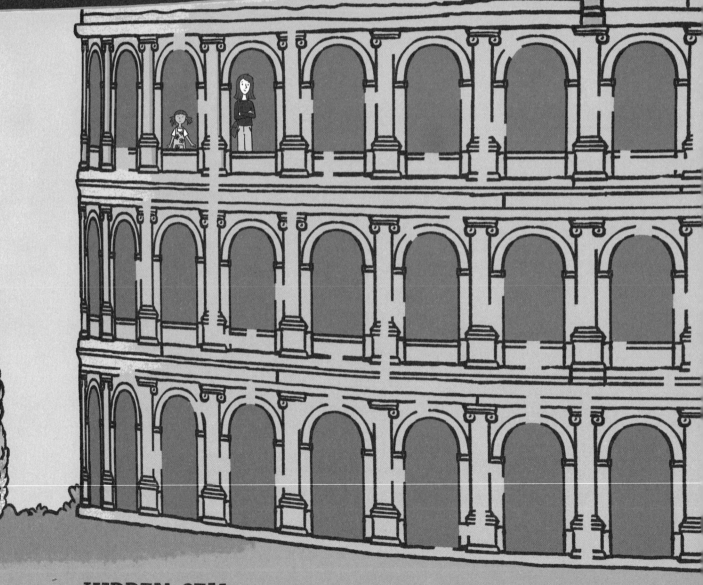

AMELIA: Hey Marco! How did it go at Hohenzollern?

MARCO: Awesome! I found Geronimo's lederhosen.

AMELIA: Excellent! Now on to Rome to meet Luca Boselli. He modeled for Geronimo. He works at the Colosseum and will be dressed as a gladiator.

MARCO: A gladiator? Cool! Heading there now.

HIDDEN GEM In the 1500s, Pope Sixtus V of Rome attempted to turn the Colosseum into an enormous wool factory. His plans proved too expensive, and work on the project ended not long after he died.

GET THAT GLADIATOR!

The Colosseum in Rome was built nearly 2,000 years ago by the emperor, Vespasian. The building was opened in AD 80 by his son, Titus, who held games to celebrate that lasted for 100 days. The games featured contests between specially trained fighters, called gladiators, who fought to the death.

END HERE!

FLUMMOX RATING
5
Stuck? Solution on Page 89

START HERE!

Help Marco through the columns and windows at the Colosseum to find Luca Boselli.

FLUMMOX RATING
1
Stuck? Solution on Page 89

END HERE!

HIDDEN GEM
The tomato, called pomodoro in Italy, didn't feature in Italian cooking until the 16th century, when it was first brought over from the Americas.

PALAVER AT THE PARTHENON

MARCO: I have Geronimo's sunglasses!

AMELIA: That's great! Now head to the Parthenon in Athens, Greece. Geronimo can't remember seeing his light reflector since he used it on his shoot there with Luca.

MARCO: We're on our way.

The Parthenon is the remains of a temple dedicated to the ancient Greek goddess Athena. The temple was built in the 5th century BC and stands on the hill of the Acropolis.

Help Marco and Luca scramble over the temple ruins to discover what Geronimo mislaid.

START HERE!

FLUMMOX RATING
3
Stuck? Solution on Page 90

END HERE!

HIDDEN GEM
People have lived in the city of Athens for over 3,000 years, making it one of the oldest cities in the world.

MARCO: We found the light reflector.

AMELIA: That's great! How do you feel about dancing? Geronimo went to a tourist performance of the Whirling Dervishes in Istanbul, Turkey. Can you go and see if he dropped anything there?

MARCO: Of course, I'm always in the mood for dancing!

START HERE!

Help Marco pick his way through the Whirling Dervishes to find what fell out of Geronimo's bag.

TURKISH WHIRL

Istanbul is the only city in the world that crosses two continents: Europe and Asia. Although it is not the capital of modern Turkey, Istanbul (formerly known as Constantinople) was the capital of three empires: the Roman, Ottoman, and Byzantine.

FLUMMOX RATING
4
Stuck? Solution on Page 90

HIDDEN GEM
The Whirling Dervishes are a part of the Sufi branch of the Islamic faith. Their whirling is a form of meditation that they believe brings them closer to God.

END HERE!

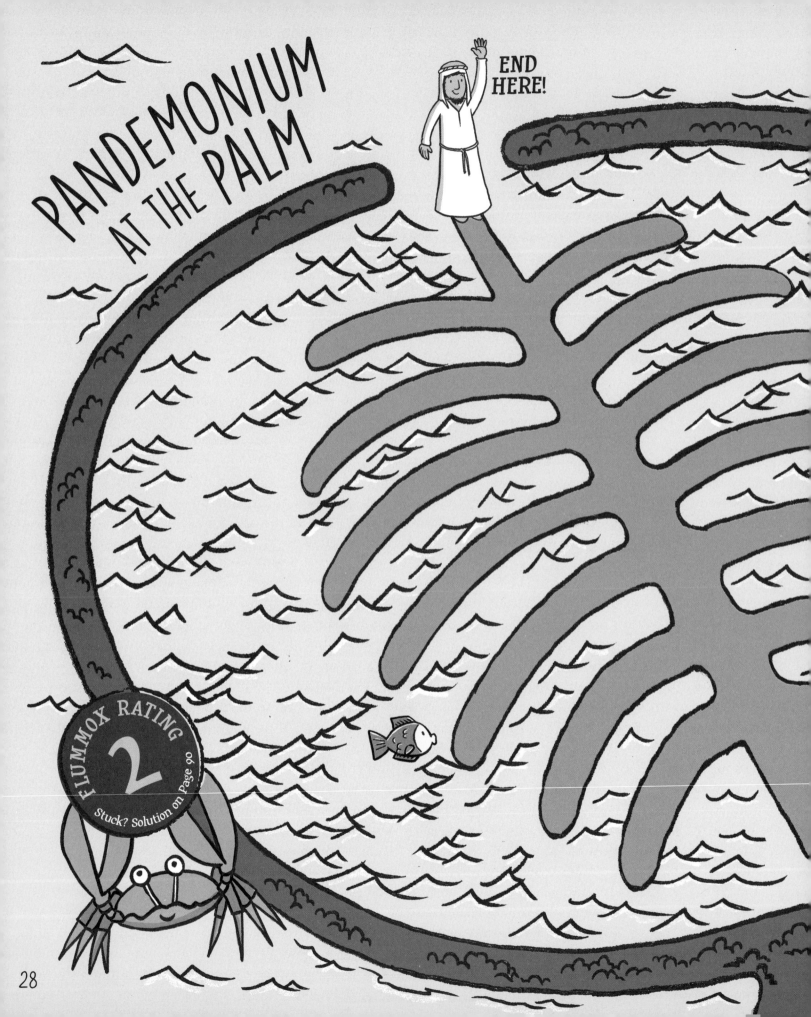

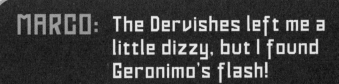

MARCO: The Dervishes left me a little dizzy, but I found Geronimo's flash!

AMELIA: Hooray! Now I need you to find Hakim Najeh, Geronimo's climbing buddy. He lives on the Palm Islands in Dubai and will take you up the Burj Khalifa.

The Palm Islands in the United Arab Emirates are made up of the three largest artificial islands on Earth. They were formed from millions of tons of sand and rock dredged up from the seafloor and are connected by a monorail and an undersea highway.

HIDDEN GEM

Developers have sunk two fighter jets off the shore in order to create an artificial coral reef.

Help Marco navigate the waves around the Palm Islands in Dubai to find Geronimo's friend, Hakim Najeh.

START HERE!

HIDDEN GEM

The Burj Khalifa has over 17,000 doors and can hold up to 35,000 people - the equivalent of a small town!

END HERE!

FLUMMOX RATING

4

Stuck? Solution on Page 96

CLIMBING THE BURJ KHALIFA

START HERE!

Towering over the city of Dubai at nearly 2,725 feet (830 m) tall, the Burj Khalifa is the tallest skyscraper in the world. It has 160 stories and is home to the world's highest restaurant.

Help Marco and Hakim make their way up and down the world's tallest building. Can you see if Geronimo lost anything on his climb?

HAKIM
Geronimo and I had an incredible climb up the Burj Khalifa.

MARCO
Geronimo must have been distracted by the view – he thinks he dropped something. It must be waaaay down there! Let's check it out.

FISHY FINDS

Dar es Salaam is
the largest city in Tanzania.
Situated on the east coast
of the country, its name means
"harbor of peace" in Arabic.

CABIN FEVER

MARCO
Hello Neema! My name is Marco. I was sent here by your photographer friend, Geronimo Keats, to look for some of his lost possessions.

NEEMA
Nice to meet you! Yes, Geronimo was here. We took a ship to Madagascar to visit the lemurs. I'll take you there.

Help Marco and Neema get through the cargo hold to find their cabins on the busy ship.

START HERE!

FLUMMOX RATING
2
Stuck? Solution on Page 91

HIDDEN GEM

Some busy cargo ships travel the equivalent of three-quarters of the way to the moon in a single year.

END HERE!

LOST AMONG THE LEMURS

NEEMA
The staff at the lemur sanctuary just told me one of the lemurs has been seen wearing a hat, but they haven't been able to catch him.

MARCO
It could belong to Geronimo. What are we waiting for? Let's check it out.

START HERE! →

Help Neema and Marco loop their way through the lemurs to find the one wearing Geronimo's hat.

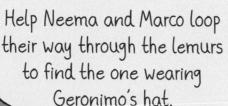

HIDDEN GEM
A male ring-tailed lemur defends his territory by rubbing his tail against his scent glands to make a stink, and then waving it at other males while yelling loudly!

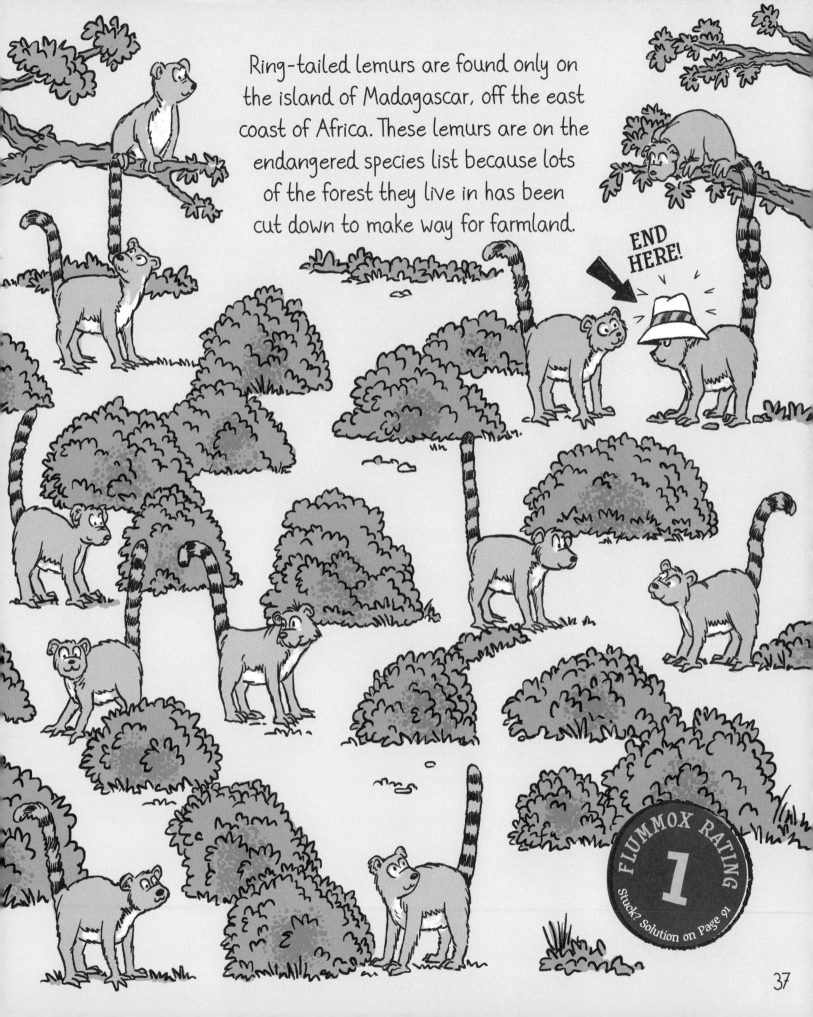

Ring-tailed lemurs are found only on the island of Madagascar, off the east coast of Africa. These lemurs are on the endangered species list because lots of the forest they live in has been cut down to make way for farmland.

END HERE!

FLUMMOX RATING
1
Stuck? Solution on Page 91

STREET—FOOD SLALOM

MARCO: We found Geronimo's hat!

AMELIA: That's great! I bet you've worked up an appetite with all this hard work.

MARCO: Now you mention it, I am pretty hungry.

AMELIA: Perfect. I need you to meet Geronimo's friend Amar at a restaurant on Jalan Alor in Kuala Lumpur, Malaysia. He will take you to the Batu Caves, where he and Geronimo went caving.

FLUMMOX RATING
3
Stuck? Solution on Page 91

Kuala Lumpur is the capital city of Malaysia. Known as KL to people who live there, Kuala Lumpur is famous for its food. Everywhere you go you are surrounded by the delicious smells of spicy curries, fragrant broths, and roasting meats.

END HERE!

HIDDEN GEM
When Kuala Lumpur was first founded, it was a small village in the middle of a tropical jungle. Now it's a modern, international city filled with skyscrapers!

Weave in and out of the food market to find Amar.

START HERE!

The Batu Caves are a network of natural limestone caves that have been transformed into a complex of holy Hindu temples. The caves attract thousands of tourists and worshippers each year, as well as lots and lots of very curious macaque monkeys.

FLUMMOX RATING
3
Stuck? Solution on Page 91

END HERE!

HIDDEN GEM
The Batu Caves are also home to a rare species of trapdoor spider that spends its whole life deep within the caves. Instead of a web, it builds a tunnel-like nest and waits for its prey to brush against the doorway.

Hotfoot it around the Hindu temple to discover what Geronimo dropped. Watch out for those meddlesome monkeys!

START HERE!

MUDDLE THROUGH MANILA

AMELIA: How's it going, Marco?

MARCO: Great. I found Geronimo's fan. Where next?

AMELIA: Make your way to Manila in the Philippines. I need you to find Gerry Mendoza at his photography stall in a market outside the city. Geronimo bought a telephoto lens there. Gerry will take you on to the Batad rice terraces.

The Philippines is made up of 7,107 tropical islands between the South China Sea and the Pacific Ocean. Its capital city, Manila, is on the largest of the islands, Luzon, and is home to over 12 million people.

START HERE!

Join Marco on his journey through Manila's busy market to find Gerry's store.

HIDDEN GEM
Jeepneys are a popular form of transportation in the Philippines and are often highly decorated. Themes have included the British royal family!

GM

END HERE!

43

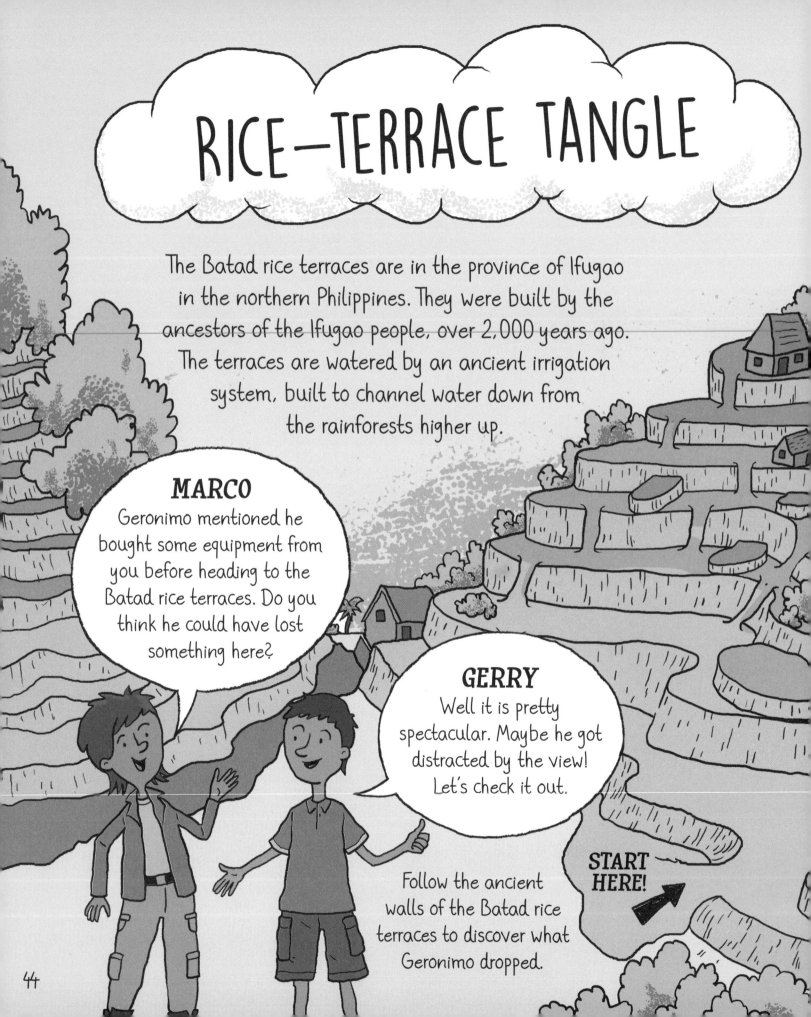

HIDDEN GEM

It is estimated that if the stone walls of the Batad rice terraces were laid end to end, they would stretch halfway around the world!

END HERE!

FLUMMOX RATING

3

Stuck? Solution on Page 91

45

LOST IN THE GILIS

FLUMMOX RATING

3

Stuck? Solution on Page 92

HIDDEN GEM

The word *gili* means "small island" in Sasak, the language of Lombok, Indonesia.

The Gili Islands - Gili Trawangan, Gili Air, and Gili Meno - are a peaceful paradise found off the coast of Lombok, Indonesia. Each of the islands has white sandy beaches and palm trees and is surrounded by coral reefs. No cars, motorbikes, or buses are allowed. If you want to get around, you can cycle, walk, or take a horse and cart!

FLUMMOX RATING
2
Stuck? Solution on Page 92

END HERE!

HIDDEN GEM

Two endangered species of turtle are found around the Gili Islands, the hawksbill turtle and the green sea turtle.

SILLY GILI SEARCH

Guide Marco and Melissa around the reef, without touching any of the delicate coral or sea turtles, to discover what Geronimo mislaid.

START HERE!

MARCO

Geronimo thinks that he may have lost something when he was on the reef.

MELISSA

Let's take a look. We divers use a lot of equipment. It's pretty easy to drop something if you aren't careful.

AMELIA: Nice work on the underwater camera, Marco!

MARCO: Thanks. Where next?

AMELIA: I need you to meet up with Geronimo's nephew, Stevie Sinclair, who will take you to Tasmania. He is currently performing at the Sydney Opera House!

MARCO: Wow! On my way.

Help Marco through the Sydney Opera House to find Geronimo's nephew, Stevie Sinclair.

START HERE!

Standing by the water in Sydney Harbor, the Sydney Opera House was designed to look like the billowing sails on a ship. Work started on the Opera House in 1959. It took over 10,000 builders to complete it.

50

ALL AROUND THE OPERA HOUSE

END HERE!

FLUMMOX RATING

5

Stuck? Solution on Page 92

HIDDEN GEM

The Sydney Opera House is home to seven music venues and can host 3,000 events each year.

The rising sea levels, caused by melting glaciers 12,000 years ago, cut the island of Tasmania off from the rest of Australia. Because of this isolation, Tasmania is home to some unique plants and animals, including the Tasmanian devil.

FLUMMOX RATING
3
Stuck? Solution on Page 92

HIDDEN GEM
The Tasmanian devil is a marsupial. Just like kangaroos, female devils have pouches to carry their young.

Tread carefully through the tangle of Tasmanian devils to discover what Geronimo left behind.

START HERE!

The township of Rotorua, situated on New Zealand's North Island, is famous for its hot springs. Rotorua has been volcanically active for many thousands of years. It is so active that some houses in the area come with their very own thermal pool in the garden.

HIDDEN GEM
Rotorua is nicknamed "Sulphur City" because of the stinky gases released by the hot springs. Ewww!

END HERE!

FLUMMOX RATING
4
Stuck? Solution on Page 92

ICE STORM!

Help Marco's plane weave in and out of the ice storm to land safely on the Ross Ice Shelf in Antarctica.

START HERE!

AMELIA: I hope you warmed yourself in the springs. Things will get very cold now!

MARCO: What do you mean?

AMELIA: I need you to fly to Antarctica. We've heard from Professor Coldsnap that there have been sightings of a penguin wearing a hat!

MARCO: What is it with animals and Geronimo's hats?!

The coldest temperature ever measured on Earth was a thermometer-shattering -128.6°F (-89.2°C) at Vostok Station, Antarctica, in 1983.

FLUMMOX RATING 4
Stuck? Solution on Page 93

HIDDEN GEM

Ninety percent of the ice on Earth is found in Antarctica, but because the continent gets so little rain, Antarctica is technically a desert.

END HERE!

Antarctica is home to 7 of the world's 17 species of penguin. The emperor penguin is the largest and also the hardiest, enduring hurricane-force winds and temperatures of -40°F (-40°C).

END HERE!

FLUMMOX RATING

2

Stuck? Solution on Page 93

HIDDEN GEM
All of the world's wild penguins live in the Southern Hemisphere. Polar bears live in the Northern Hemisphere.

IN AND OUT OF THE ICEBERGS

MARCO: Hi Amelia, I got the hat! I hope Pom-Pom isn't cold without it.

AMELIA: I'm sure he's used to it. Ok, I hope you've got your sea legs. I need you to sail around Cape Horn, Chile, and up to Robinson Crusoe Island.

MARCO: OK. Hopefully I won't get marooned!

FLUMMOX RATING
3
Stuck? Solution on Page 93

START HERE!

Help Marco navigate the treacherous waters around Cape Horn to sail up the coast of Chile and reach Robinson Crusoe Island.

The icebergs and the strong waves and currents around Cape Horn, Chile, make it a very dangerous place to sail, but many modern sailors can't resist the challenge.

END HERE!

HIDDEN GEM
Jakob Le Maire and Willem Schouten from the Netherlands were the first sailors to successfully navigate Cape Horn, in 1616.

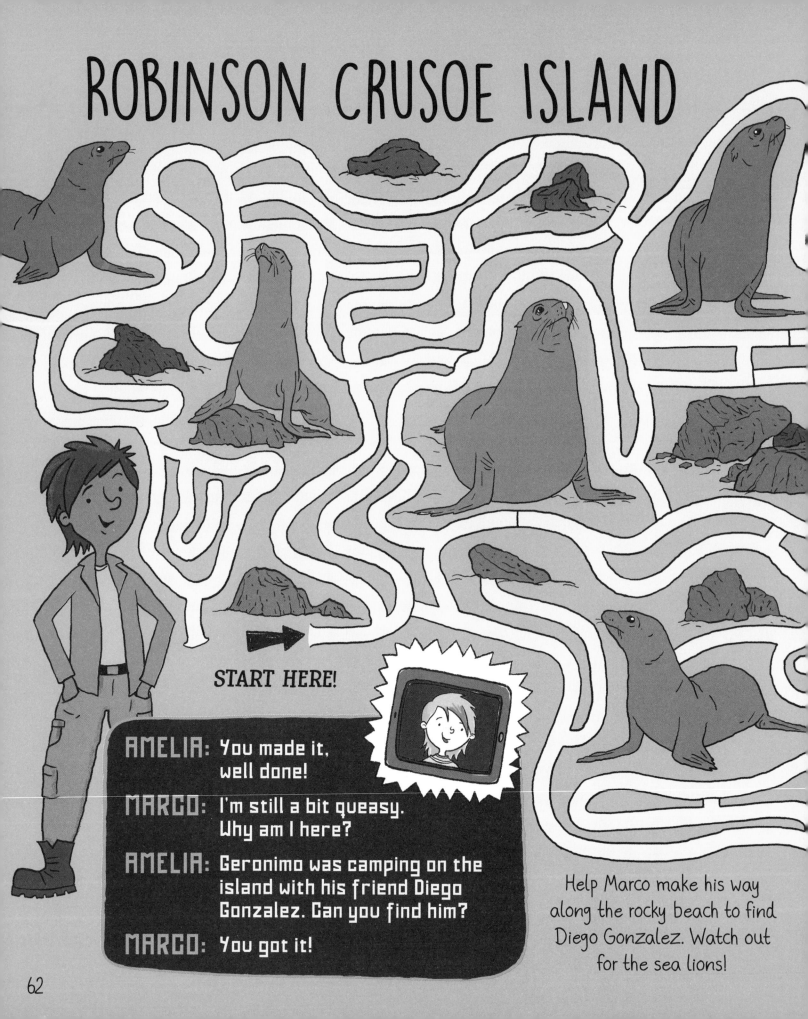

ROBINSON CRUSOE ISLAND

START HERE!

AMELIA: You made it, well done!

MARCO: I'm still a bit queasy. Why am I here?

AMELIA: Geronimo was camping on the island with his friend Diego Gonzalez. Can you find him?

MARCO: You got it!

Help Marco make his way along the rocky beach to find Diego Gonzalez. Watch out for the sea lions!

Robinson Crusoe Island is named after the famous book by Daniel Defoe. It tells the story of a man shipwrecked on a deserted island for 28 years, and was based on a real castaway called Alexander Selkirk.

END HERE!

FLUMMOX RATING
3
Stuck? Solution on Page 93

HIDDEN GEM
Alexander Selkirk spent five years on the island after demanding to put ashore in 1704 because he believed the ship he was on would sink. He was right - it did!

NAVIGATE THE NAZCA LINES

The Nazca Lines are geometric designs and pictures carved into the desert, and cover about 174 square miles (450 sq km). They were created by an ancient civilization called the Nazca between 500 BC and AD 500. Most of the designs are so big they are impossible to make out from the ground.

FLUMMOX RATING
3
Stuck? Solution on Page 93

END HERE!

MARCO: I found Geronimo's water canteen! Where next?

AMELIA: I want you to go and meet Geronimo's submariner friend, Milton Burgess. He's on vacation in Barbados. He will take you to the Great Blue Hole in Belize.

MARCO: You mean I'm going on a submarine trip? Awesome. This sounds like my kind of mission. Count me in!

START HERE!

FLUMMOX RATING

1

Stuck? Solution on Page 93

Help Marco make his way through the palm trees and hammocks to find Geronimo's friend.

CARIBBEAN COOL

Barbados is the most easterly of the 700 islands that make up the Caribbean. It is very popular with tourists due to its warm tropical weather, clear seas, and white sandy beaches.

END HERE!

HIDDEN GEM

Mount Hillaby is the highest point in Barbados, but at 1,115 feet (340 m), it's less than half the height of the world's tallest building!

HIDDEN GEM

The Great Blue Hole was originally a huge cave on dry land. The ceiling collapsed due to erosion, and the sinkhole was submerged when sea levels rose.

END HERE!

68

PIE TIME!

The Florida Keys are a group of tropical islands off the coast of southern Florida. Key lime pie, a popular dessert, was first made here over 100 years ago.

MARCO: That was amazing! And we found Geronimo's fish ID guide.

AMELIA: Great! Did you work up an appetite?

MARCO: I am pretty hungry.

AMELIA: You've definitely earned a treat. Head to the Key Lime Pie Factory in Key Largo, Florida. You need to find Brad McCabe. Then his son, Kendall, will take you on to the Everglades.

START HERE!

Help Marco wind his way through the pie production line to find the factory's owner, Brad McCabe.

SWAMP SCRAMBLE

MARCO
Hi Kendall! Geronimo Keats thinks he may have lost something while he was with you in the Everglades. Can you help me track it down?

KENDALL
Great to meet you! Geronimo and I photographed alligators together while we were in the Everglades. Let's go and see what we can find!

START HERE!

Help Marco and Kendall weave their airboat around the chomping alligators to find Geronimo's headphones.

The Everglades National Park is a tropical wetland that covers 2,410 square miles (6,241 sq km) in southern Florida. It was made a national park in 1947 and is a unique ecosystem that is home to 14 endangered species - and lots of alligators!

END HERE!

HIDDEN GEM
Airboats are perfect for navigating the shallow Everglades because of their flat bottoms. They are propelled by a huge fan that sits above the water.

FLUMMOX RATING
1
Stuck? Solution on Page 94

FLUMMOX RATING 3
Stuck? Solution on Page 94

The Grand Canyon in Arizona was carved out by the Colorado River. It is 277 miles (446 km) long, up to 1.1 miles (1.8 km) deep, and up to 18 miles (29 km) wide.

END HERE!

HIDDEN GEM

The limestone at the rim of the canyon is around 230 million years old. The layers of rock get steadily older until you reach the bottom, where the schist rock is over two billion years old.

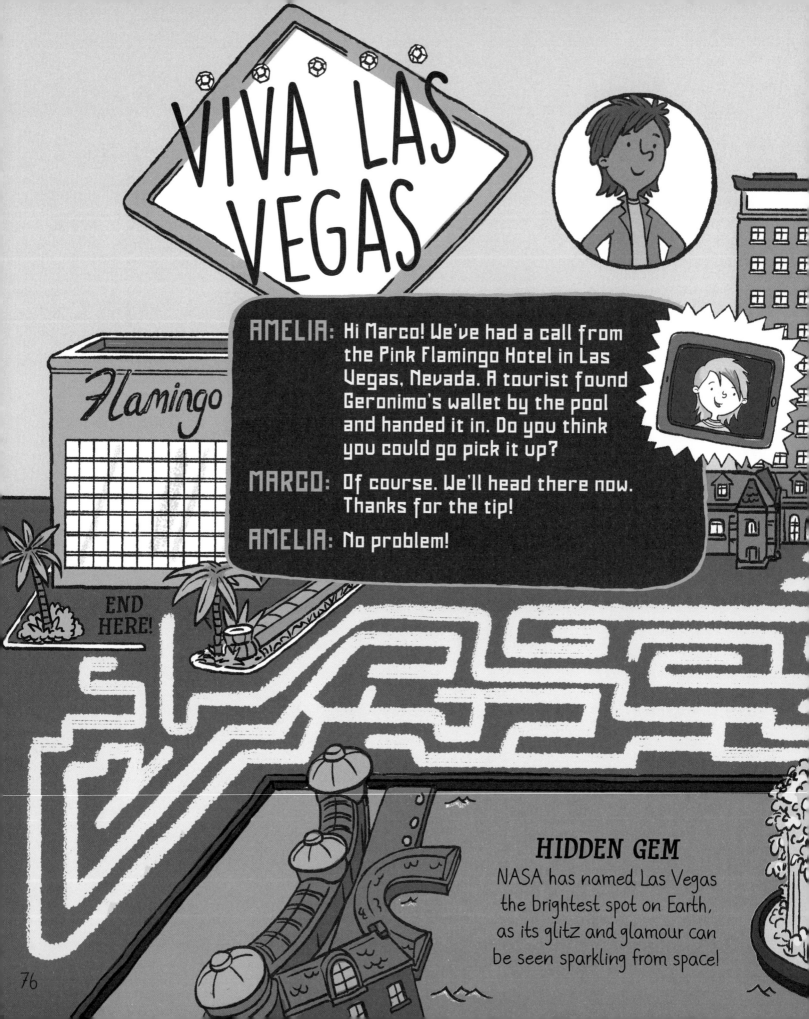

VIVA LAS VEGAS

AMELIA: Hi Marco! We've had a call from the Pink Flamingo Hotel in Las Vegas, Nevada. A tourist found Geronimo's wallet by the pool and handed it in. Do you think you could go pick it up?

MARCO: Of course. We'll head there now. Thanks for the tip!

AMELIA: No problem!

END HERE!

HIDDEN GEM
NASA has named Las Vegas the brightest spot on Earth, as its glitz and glamour can be seen sparkling from space!

FLUMMOX RATING 2
Stuck? Solution on Page 94

Las Vegas, in the US state of Nevada, has replicas of all kinds of tourist attractions from around the world. The only thing it doesn't have is rainfall. Las Vegas is in the middle of the Mojave Desert and only gets 4 inches (10 cm) of rain a year.

START HERE!

Help Kendall and Marco stroll up and down the Strip to find the Pink Flamingo Hotel and Geronimo's lost wallet.

IN A LATHER AT OLD FAITHFUL

Help Marco avoid the bears and bison in Yellowstone National Park and discover what Geronimo lost in the geyser.

FLUMMOX RATING
1
Stuck? Solution on Page 95

When the first European person visited Yellowstone and returned with stories of gushing geysers and multicolored pools, people dismissed his tales as wild exaggeration. They were wrong. Yellowstone's unique volcanic landscape led to it becoming the world's first national park, in 1872.

END HERE!

HIDDEN GEM
Old Faithful is the most reliable thermal feature in the world. It erupts roughly every 90 minutes.

FLUMMOX RATING 3 Stuck? Solution on Page 95

Two million people visit Whistler, Canada, every year to enjoy the majestic mountains, over 200 exciting ski and snowboard trails, and of course the snow. Whistler gets over 36 feet (11 m) of snow a year.

END HERE!

HIDDEN GEM
Whistler is named after a ground squirrel that makes a high-pitched warning call when it senses danger.

FUN AT THE FALLS

MARCO: Got the goggles! That was a fun ride.

AMELIA: Well done! We're almost done. Just one more stop – Niagara Falls! You might want to take your raincoat.

MARCO: I'm on my way.

START HERE!

Help Marco find his way through the spray to discover what Geronimo mislaid.

Niagara Falls is in fact three separate waterfalls: American Falls, Horseshoe Falls, and Bridal Veil Falls. Horseshoe Falls, the largest of the three, lies mostly in Canada, whereas Bridal Veil Falls and the aptly named American Falls are on the American side.

FLUMMOX RATING

4

Stuck? Solution on Page 95

END HERE!

HIDDEN GEM
More than 3,483 tons of water flow over Niagara Falls every second. That's over a million bathtubs!

Oxford Street in London is the busiest shopping street in Europe. It is about 1.2 miles (2 km) long and attracts shoppers and tourists from all over the world.

FLUMMOX RATING
4
Stuck? Solution on Page 95

HIDDEN GEM

Oxford Street used to be called Tyburn Road and was the road that linked the infamous Newgate Prison to a set of gallows called the Tyburn Tree, close to where Marble Arch stands today. It is thought that in total over 40,000 people were executed there.

END HERE!

DOUBLE-DECKER DIVERSION

MARCO: Hi Amelia! I've got all of Geronimo's lost items and picked up his new suitcases – I'm heading back!

AMELIA: Yay! That's fab. Geronimo is with me now, so why don't you hop on the bus and meet us at Lonely Planet HQ.

MARCO: I'm on my way.

START HERE!

Help Marco navigate the London bus routes to reach the Lonely Planet HQ on the South Bank.

END HERE!

HIDDEN GEM
Some very unusual items end up at Transport for London's lost and found, including a preserved pufferfish and false teeth!

FLUMMOX RATING
2
Stuck? Solution on Page 95

Marco's MAZE SOLUTIONS

PAGES 4–23

PAGES 4–5: SECURITY SLALOM

PAGES 6–7: VIGELAND ADVENTURE!

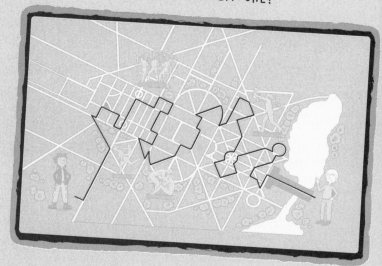

PAGES 8–9: FAST FJORD–WARD

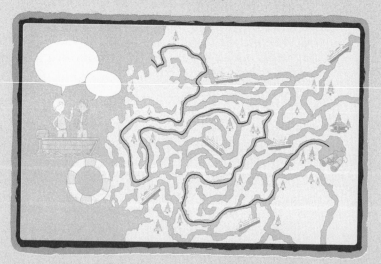

PAGES 10–11: METRO MAYHEM

PAGES 12-13: CATHEDRAL CAPER

PAGES 14-15: CHOCOLATE TIME

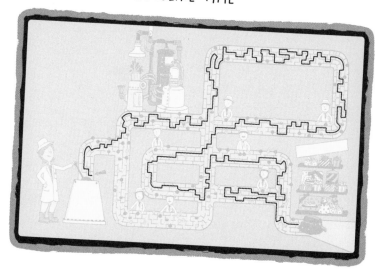

PAGES 16-17: FOREST FORAY!

PAGES 18-19: TURRET TANGLE

PAGES 20-21: GET THAT GLADIATOR!

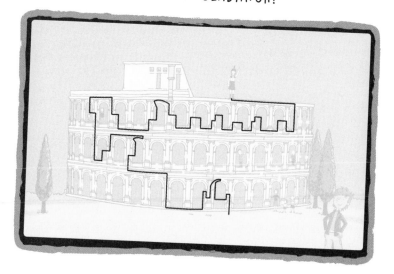

PAGES 22-23: PIZZA IN THE PIAZZA!

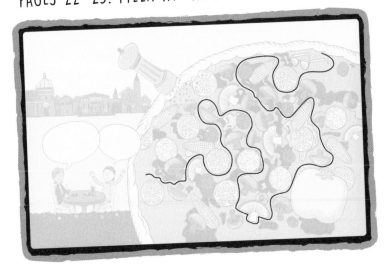

Marco's MAZE SOLUTIONS
PAGES 24–45

PAGES 24–25: PALAVER AT THE PARTHENON

PAGES 26–27: TURKISH WHIRL

PAGES 28–29: PANDEMONIUM AT THE PALM

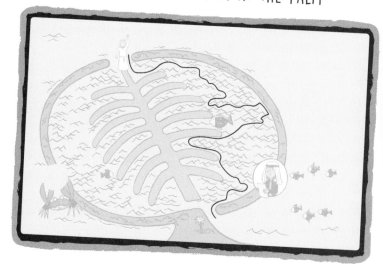

PAGES 30–31: CLIMBING THE BURJ KHALIFA

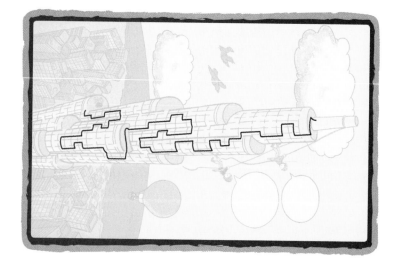

PAGES 32–33: FISHY FINDS

PAGES 34–35: CABIN FEVER

PAGES 36–37: LOST AMONG THE LEMURS

PAGES 38–39: STREET–FOOD SLALOM

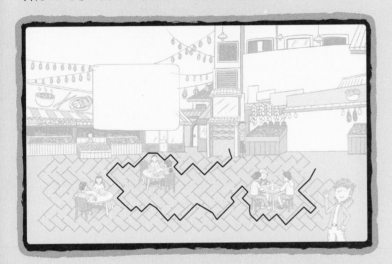

PAGES 40–41: MACAQUE MONKEY MADNESS

PAGES 42–43: MUDDLE THROUGH MANILA

PAGES 44–45: RICE–TERRACE TANGLE

Marco's MAZE SOLUTIONS

PAGES 46–67

PAGES 46–47: LOST IN THE GILIS

PAGES 48–49: SILLY GILI SEARCH

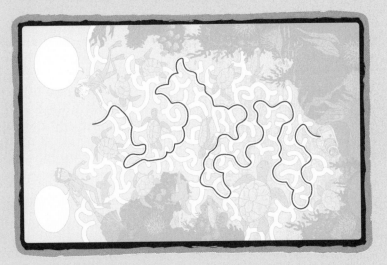

PAGES 50–51: ALL AROUND THE OPERA HOUSE

PAGES 52–53: DARTING AMONG THE DEVILS

PAGES 54–55: RUSH AROUND ROTORUA

PAGES 56–57: ICE STORM!

PAGES 58–59: THE SEARCH FOR POM-POM

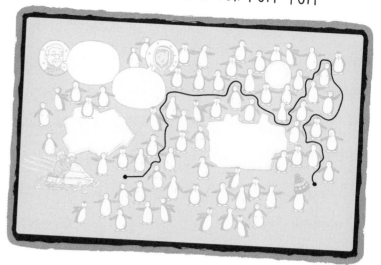

PAGES 60–61: IN AND OUT OF THE ICEBERGS

PAGES 62–63: ROBINSON CRUSOE ISLAND

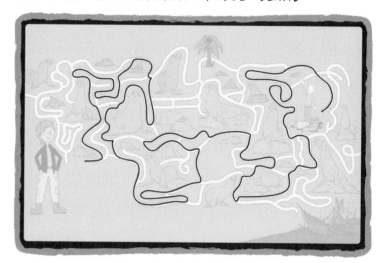

PAGES 64–65: NAVIGATE THE NAZCA LINES

PAGES 66–67: CARIBBEAN COOL

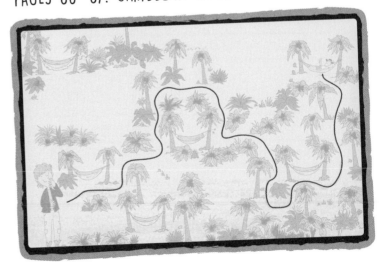

Marco's MAZE SOLUTIONS

PAGES 68–86

PAGES 68–69: INTO THE GREAT BLUE HOLE

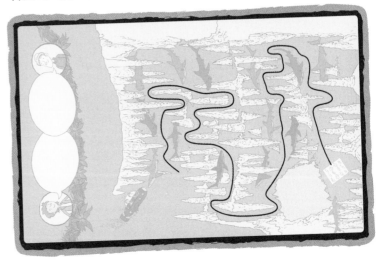

PAGES 70–71: PIE TIME!

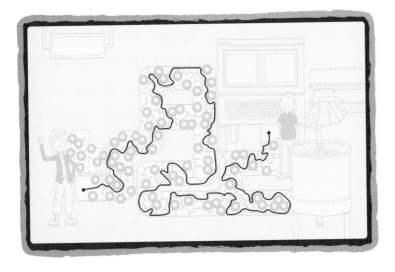

PAGES 72–73: SWAMP SCRAMBLE

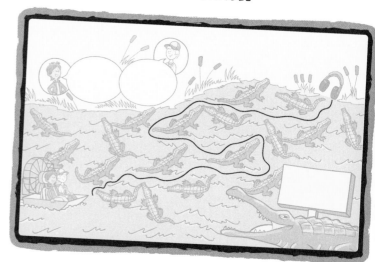

PAGES 74–75: GRAND CANYON CAPER

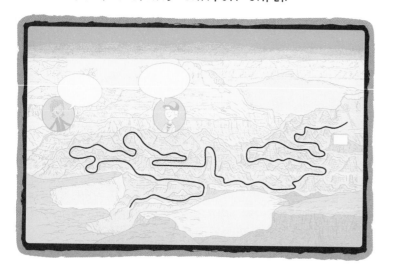

PAGES 76–77: VIVA LAS VEGAS

PAGES 78–79: IN A LATHER AT OLD FAITHFUL

PAGES 80–81: SWOOSH, THERE IT IS!

PAGES 82–83: FUN AT THE FALLS

PAGES 84–85: ON THE CASE

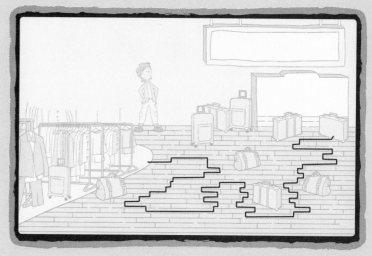

PAGES 86: DOUBLE-DECKER DIVERSION

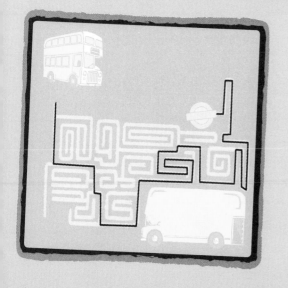

Marco's MAZE ADVENTURE

Published in May 2017
by Lonely Planet Global Limited
CRN: 554153
ISBN: 978 1 78657 687 3
www.lonelyplanetkids.com
© Lonely Planet 2017

10 9 8 7 6 5 4 3 2 1

Printed in China

Commissioned and project managed by Dynamo Limited
Author: Jane Gledhill
Editor: Dynamo Limited
Design: Dynamo Limited
Illustration: Dynamo Limited
Publishing Director: Piers Pickard
Publisher: Tim Cook
Commissioning Editors: Jen Feroze and Catharine Robertson
Print production: Larissa Frost and Nigel Longuet

With thanks to: Jennifer Dixon and Christina Webb

LONELY PLANET OFFICES

STAY IN TOUCH
lonelyplanet.com/contact

AUSTRALIA
The Malt Store, Level 3, 551 Swanston St., Carlton, Victoria 3053
T: 03 8379 8000

IRELAND
Unit E, Digital Court, The Digital Hub,
Rainsford St., Dublin 8

USA
124 Linden St., Oakland, CA 94607
T: 510 250 6400

UK
240 Blackfriars Rd., London SE1 8NW
T: 020 3771 5100